valentine.

Wynnie Valentine

In loving memory of Mrs. Reed

-for my friends, family, and whoever I become-

This is my story.

CONTENTS

Why do I write?

No matter the amount of time I've spent writing,

I always have more to express.

I'm tempted to believe my possibilities are endless.

"Why do you write?" An ex once asked me.

I get that question a lot,

But whenever someone asks me that,

I always seem to give a different answer.

For him, I wanted this answer to be specifically creative.

At first, I was silent.

I had to give it a moment of thought.

"Why create any form of art?" I asked back.

"Expression," he answered — not too sure of himself. "Right?"

"Why do a puzzle?" I asked.

He tilted his head and shrugged his shoulders.

"Words are puzzle pieces," I said. "Except, there's no singular outcome."

"You get to make whatever you want," he added.

I nodded. "It just depends on how you put them together."

He smiled. "Anyone can put a puzzle together — eventually at least..."

"...But not everyone can use the pieces to make

Something completely unique and original."

— Wynnie Valentine

Emotion.

I'm too emotional.

I've always had a heavy heart.

Perhaps *too* heavy.

But when each emotion is

A reminder that I am alive,

What is life without *feeling*?

God, if I were numb and emotionless,

I wouldn't wish to walk the earth at all.

Living is to *embrace.*

To feel the warmth of the sun,

And the chill of a winter's night.

Each tear, each smile:

A testament to the miles I've walked.

In both joy and in sorrow,

I further discover the essence of

What it means to *live*.

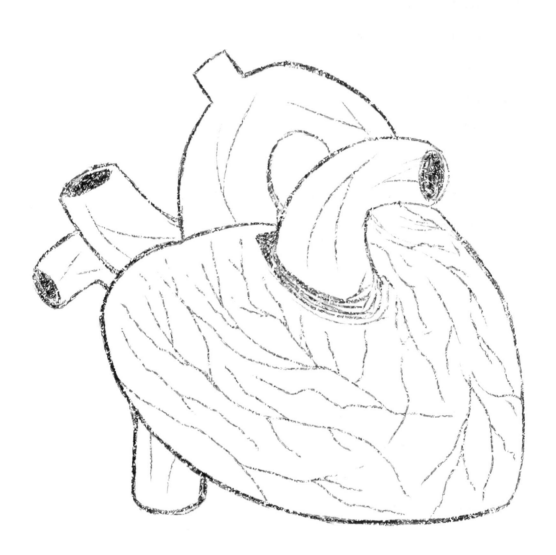

I'm a teenager.

Though I have not lived for long,

I've already come to learn that:

In a world like this,

Voices like mine are meant to be silenced.

I know — I won't be heard until I'm loud enough,

But sometimes,

Even screaming at the top of my lungs is

Nothing but a whisper among what others have to say.

Once my throat bleeds dry,

I shut my mouth and carry on.

I'm often stubborn.

I've never been one to

Admit when I'm wrong.

I'm getting better at that.

For as long as I can remember,

Pride has had a firm grip on my soul.

I let it hold me down — hold me back.

I used to argue with people.

I hated that.

No one notices, but I'm quieter now.

I *try* to mind my business and keep to myself.

My voice doesn't feel invalid as long as I don't have one.

Things aren't as simple as they used to be.

When I was little, I felt emotion,

But not to the point of

Panic attacks and suicide attempts.

I'm still as naive as I've always been,

Except without nap times and recesses.

Those things of simple joys have been replaced with

Responsibilities and relationships to manage.

The truth is, I just don't know how to act.

I want to be an innocent little girl,

But that's obviously too far behind me.

I try to be mature,

But I'm often told that

I'm too ahead of myself.

I'm clueless —

Inclosed in a blurry box of questions.

I should speak up and ask,

But I'd hate to seem behind.

I want to be normal.

I want to do good.

I crave guidance in a way that

Doesn't rip my inner child to pieces.

I'm grateful.

I certainly don't show it enough,

But I *am* grateful for everything around me.

I love my home, and I think about it a lot;

Especially when I think about killing myself.

I cry in the shower thinking about how privileged I am.

Jerk. Loser. Brat. I call myself. *I hate my life.*

But I don't hate my life,

I just hate the way I've lived it.

I hate my past.

I'm in pain.

My actions have brought me to a wicked place.

I can't seem to fade the scars of wounds

That I used to think were only scrapes.

Really, they were cuts,

So deep into my chest that

My heart had been removed,

And taken from me.

You'd think that a person would

Realize that they were being cut open;

Gushing from the inside out.

Yet I didn't notice.

Not at all.

I'm a writer.

I have my way with words,

Yet all I've known is silence.

Unsaid thoughts tear my mind to pieces.

I put them on paper — praying that they'll leave.

Instead, I've brought them to life.

I've kept secrets for far too long.

If a ghost like this one refuses to leave me,

Then why not share it with the world?

I know that my parents will disapprove of this story.

I'm positive that they love me,

But during my teenage years,

They've never *truly* known me.

It's no one's fault but my own.

I never *let* them.

I *don't* open up enough,

And when I do,

I feel unheard and misunderstood.

Because of this,

I've hidden a lot of things;

Things that I regret.

Things that I *should* have told somebody.

Poetry.

I found poetry in the eighth grade.

We only spent a few weeks covering it,

But my English teacher always

Encouraged me to continue writing.

Her classroom was where my passion really began.

She was a motivational speaker,

And inspired me to find my voice.

Through my stormy seas,

She was a lighthouse — built to guide the way.

I was lucky enough to be one of her last students.

She held a book club that all of my friends were in.

As a gift to the club,

She gave out these cheap, plastic mood rings.

I still wear mine all the time — everywhere.

It's been over a year since cancer brought her to an early grave,

But I still think about her.

Deep down, she's why I still write.

We shared that same desire to make an impact with our words,

And though she can't be here to make that difference in the world,

I can only try my best to inspire others the way she did.

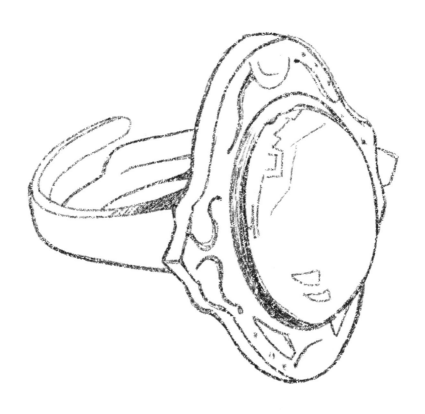

I have a hard time moving on.

I met my first *real* boyfriend in that classroom.

She sat us right next to each other.

She watched us flirt,

And playfully teased us for it.

Just to be close to me,

He joined the book club.

On the day I gave my speech,

He accompanied her in the crowd.

And when the day came,

We attended her funeral mass together...

I think a piece of me died when she passed away,

And that boy took the rest of me with him.

Without them,

I feel like a completely different person.

To me, the three of us were tied together.

I thought that when

Him and I were all grown up,

We'd go back to visit her,

But it looks like life had other plans for us.

I like to think that maybe they were both

Lessons of finding myself through **love, loss, and grief.**

He doesn't care about me anymore.

He broke up with me just before

The beginning of our sophomore year.

It didn't feel real —

Like the earth itself was collapsing onto me.

After all of those late-night talks about the future,

I had already made so many plans for us.

Now, those plans vanish into thin air,

And my life goes dry.

There's a silence where his voice used to be,

But the silence I hear isn't quiet.

It's loud sort of noise —

One that sounds like him,

Except he's no longer in the room with me.

He isn't sitting at the desk in front of me,

Or laying in my arms.

Not anymore.

Now, he only exists in the back of my mind —

Like a memory I can feel against my skin.

I know that the love I felt was real,

But now it feels like nothing but

An awful nightmare.

Grief.

I think about him a lot.

My first "love."

I wish I didn't think about him.

It's been awhile since we last spoke,

Yet he still rots in my mind as I lie in bed at night.

I remember the flowers he bought me —

How I forgot to throw them out.

Like my mind, the water fogged,

And the flowers died.

For months, they sat there wilting;

Drying up by my vanity mirror.

Whenever I looked at them, I saw myself.

Dead. Dry. Falling apart.

I tell myself, *I don't hate him,*

But that's getting harder to believe.

He deserves to be hated,

But there is no rage in me. No anger.

Just some kind of depression that has infected me.

I lie in bed and cry.

I can't seem to figure out what's wrong,

Or why I still feel so dead inside.

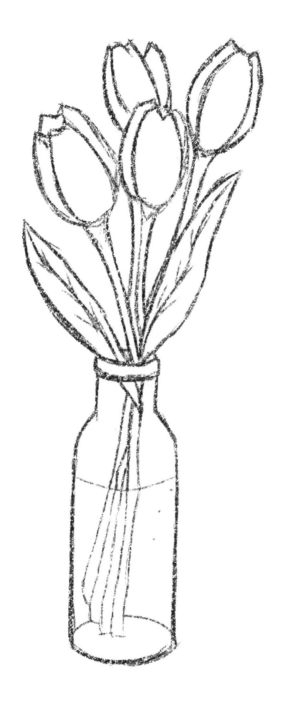

He lied and cheated.

Afterwards,

He'd lean on me and cry.

Though I was the victim,

I pitied him.

"Everyone makes mistakes,"

I'd tell him.

I'd forgive him *over and over.*

I'd convince him that

He was deserving of

Second and third chances.

I put up with all of it for *two years,*

Just for him to leave me.

That's not the way things were supposed to happen.

I was supposed to find the courage to let him go.

Instead, another girl looked his way,

And he was gone.

I know it's not my fault.

It still hurts though.

Not because I miss being with him,

But because the pain was easier to relieve when

Both of us were feeling it.

When I'm lying in my bed,

I trace over the scars he left me with.

Without his manipulation to be my drug,

I realize how bad the bleeding really was.

He knows what he's done,

And he's over with it.

He wipes the blood from his blade,

And claims that he's changed,

But I don't spot a difference.

He still looks at me.

I know he still thinks about me,

But he doesn't miss me.

I don't miss him either,

I just miss feeling loved — even if it was fake.

I miss when he'd lie and then apologize.

I miss when he'd say that I deserved better,

And that he wanted to

Be that better person.

To me, that was love.

I was naive enough to believe that one day

I'd help him to become the best version of himself,

And that we'd spend the rest of our lives together.

I still wonder what I did wrong.

I wonder why he doesn't miss me.

More importantly,

I wonder why I even care.

I know the truth:

That being a bad person is

Easier when you're single — when you don't have a

Heartbroken girlfriend sobbing into your shoulder.

I just think that something inside of me still wants to see the good in him.

Even if the apology meant that I'd be torn apart once more,

At least he used to say sorry.

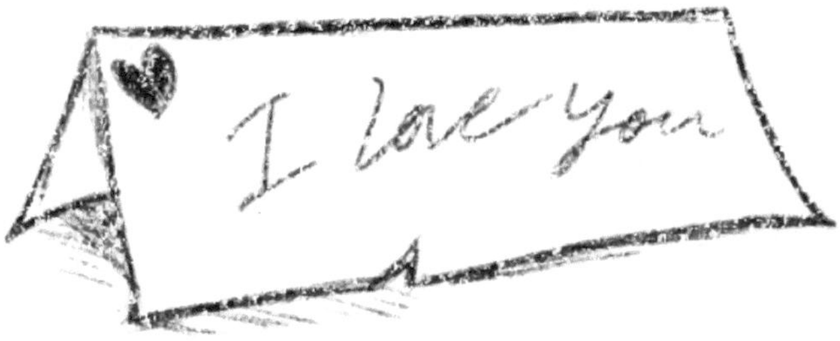
I love you

Boys.

I've dated other boys.

The memories of them blur together,

Like flashing movie scenes on a cinema screen.

"I love you."

The words burn into my skin like blazes of acid rain

Pouring down on me like the tears I once shed.

No matter how many

Random boys I involve myself with,

I can't seem to forget *him.*

Sometimes when I think of him,

I wonder if I'll ever love anyone else the same.

In many cases,

I've taught myself to "love."

Not because I had to,

But because it became a habit.

To me, love wasn't a feeling anymore,

Just more of a fact that lived within myself.

I've tried so hard to replace that feeling.

I broke up with my last boyfriend a few weeks ago.

I made the excuse that I "needed space,"

But to be completely honest,

I'm not too sure how to feel.

Because he's a junior, we went to prom together.

That night was wonderful.

He told me that he loved me —

That he wanted to be in my life forever.

He painted a perfect picture of our future together,

And I burned the canvas.

He really loved me.

I don't doubt that he was ready to give me his all.

I don't even deny that he deserved better —

That he deserved a relationship with the girl I was,

Back before I'd been dissected and

Mangled by the boy I first loved.

I wanted to be that girl for him, but how could I?

After being so betrayed,

How could I be so vulnerable with anyone else again?

That's when I realized the awful truth about myself:

That I wanted to be loved,

But wasn't yet prepared to be loved by someone new.

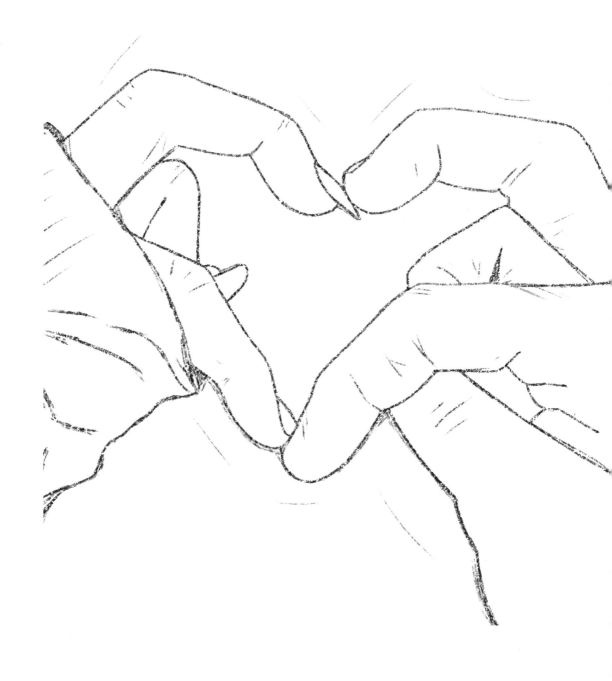

I'm too young for this.

With every boy I've ever been with,

I obsessed over the little details;

Distracting myself from the way I really felt.

When losing those boys,

I cried each time,

But not the way you cry when you lose a lover —

More like the way a mother cries once

She realizes that her son has grown taller than her.

The little boy she once knew is gone,

And in his place is an unrecognizable heap of hormones.

I begin to wonder if this is what dating is like for all teenage girls.

I should be done with relationships.

For now at least.

I'm tired of hating myself.

I'm tired of revolving my life around a single person,

Patiently waiting to find out if it's love.

I'm tired of writing cards that'll just end up in the trash.

I'm tired of wilting corsages and

Meaningless movie nights.

I'm tired of sexual pressure,

And I'm certainly tired of being touched.

Right now, I just need a friend. A kind, loyal, friend.

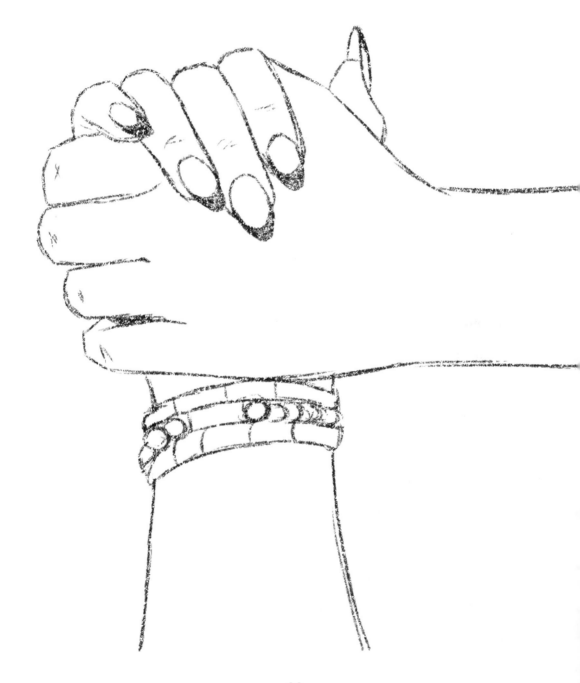

30

Relationships.

For a while, I ignored the idea of dating.

I met two boys: both a year younger than me.

When the three of us ended up in the same class,

Common interests pulled us together like magnets.

It felt like the three of us clicked — a trio.

Of course, they already knew each other well,

But it didn't take me long to catch up.

At times, I felt as if I could see right through them.

I could tell that they'd built walls around themselves —

Each brick laid with care to protect their fragile hearts.

To me, they were special.

They were different than other boys because

They'd never ask for anything more than

A friendship with me.

The sense of humor seemed to match,

And so did the intentions.

Finally, I could be myself without

The worry of someone smashing my heart to pieces.

"The trio"became a safe space.

Their words made me feel all the good things —

Things that I'd barely experienced within

Romantic relationships.

For once in my teenage life,

I didn't have to overthink who I was,

Because with them I just *knew*.

I know they felt the same with me because

They'd say things like:

"Don't tell anyone this, but–"

Or *"This is super embarrassing, but–"*

Those secrets let me know that they trusted me,

And that I could trust them too.

There was just something about the way

They'd look at me when I spoke —

A look that said, "I'm listening,"

Even if all I had to say was

Some stupid joke they'd heard before.

In a world where I felt silenced,

They made me feel heard.

Friends... Right?

Lately, the trio feels more like a duo.

One of those boys seems to

Show more interest in me than the other.

I'd known of him for a while,

But never really took the time to notice him before.

Romantically, I'm not attracted to him.

I don't see myself caring for him in *that* way,

Not yet at least.

I don't know enough about him to

Obsess over the details.

I know that I make him nervous,

And that I enjoy it.

We only talk a few times a week,

But every conversation is a connection.

I like it because it's innocent;

Because I find it unlikely that

I'll ever fall in love with him.

But beneath the surface,

I still wonder if he has real feelings for me.

I try to shake the thought from my head.

I can't do this. I should be done with relationships.

Situationships.

I shouldn't be falling for him.

I never thought I'd like him in that way —

Not in a million years.

But lately, I find myself smiling at his texts.

I catch him staring at me from across the room,

And realize that he sometimes catches me admiring him too.

As I spend more time with him,

The lines between friendship and something more begin to blur.

It's just a crush.

I don't want to date him;

Especially not right now,

But I'm smart enough to know that

There's something there.

We make eye contact, but not too often.

We touch, but not too much.

We talk, but it's not too deep —

Just deep enough to be different from any

Conversation we've ever had before.

I realize that it's officially become a *situationship.*

It's simple enough, isn't it?

People used to always tell me that

Situationships are too complicated,

And at first I couldn't see it.

There's no pressure,

Just enjoying each other's company.

All we do is play video games,

And help each other with homework.

In every confusing sort of way,

Those moments seem to matter more than

Any romantic relationship ever could.

It's a strange feeling — this budding affection.

It's like a secret I'm not too sure I want to keep,

But I'm still too afraid to share.

It's as if my heart tiptoes on

The edge of vulnerability,

Caught between

The thrill of connection,

And the fear of rejection.

I can't help the way I feel.

Every time we meet,

His presence in the room is like

A flame in the dark.

There's a spark that ignites within me —

A warmth that spreads throughout my chest.

This heat, it's like fire,

And I can't tell if it's

Keeping me safe from the cold,

Or burning me slowly.

I'm not supposed to care.

This time's different, I tell myself.

I'm not supposed to care about the way things work out.

I'm just along for the ride —

Waiting for his feelings to fade,

Or until I get bored of the thrill.

I will not — under any circumstance — fall in love with this boy.

I prepare myself to be ready for the moment he moves on,

But as the months pass, he sticks around.

It's beginning to seem like he wants something more,

But I can't quite jump to that conclusion.

Lately, he's harder to read.

He sends me mixed signals —

Sitting a few inches further away than he did yesterday,

But just last week he stepped on my foot and he kept it there

Just for the comfort of touching me somehow.

He texts me constantly,

But barely talks to me in person.

His actions should

Speak louder than his words,

Yet as of recent,

His silence is all I've heard.

He tells me that I make him nervous,

But it's not because he likes me.

Somehow, I don't believe him.

It's almost like he can't decide.

He drops hints just to pick them up again —

Sometimes ghosting me for a few weekends.

You're doing it again, I tell myself.

You're overthinking.

You're obsessed.

I'm hooked.

Situationships aren't as simple as I thought.

I was looking for a friend to casually flirt with for a while.

Instead, I find myself attached again.

Now, I can't imagine life without him.

He seems so perfect. That's what I always end up telling myself,

Even when it isn't true.

I'm obsessed again, and I know it'll pass,

But the details keep my mind locked up in a cage of daydream.

He cares about my opinion of him,

And actually laughs at my stupid jokes.

He reads the same comics as me,

And watches all the same TV shows.

We have too much in common for me *not* to obsess.

What hurts the most is that I can *feel* how close we've grown.

I know he feels it too because we only sit mere inches away.

As I'm sitting there, I realize:

It's the thrill of not knowing whether or not he likes me that

Keeps me so hooked.

And when the truth comes out —

No matter what the answer is —

I will grieve that thrill.

I know this because I've felt it before,

And I've mistaken it for love.

Birthdays.

It's my birthday.

I've just turned sixteen,

But I still feel like a little kid.

I begin to wonder if

My eighteenth birthday will feel any different.

I don't envision myself feeling like a **woman** anytime soon.

Nevertheless, I'll be an **adult** in two years.

I can't help but thinking that I won't make it—

That I'll end up dead if not in debt,

Or that I'll crash my first car before

Making it into college.

What if I make the wrong choices?

My English teacher was an optimist.

I know that she'd want me to look on the bright side,

But I'd hate to be one of those

Teenagers who thinks they're invincible—

That nothing bad will ever happen to them.

People make mistakes, and I will too.

I guess that's the optimistic way of looking at things.

Crash. Burn. Learn.

I just worry that

I'll disappoint everyone —

That I won't live up to

This image I've painted of myself.

I keep telling people that

I'll make a difference,

But what if I don't?

What if I die before getting the chance to make that big impact?

I'm afraid of a lot of things.

Someone once told me that

They admired my confidence.

Had that person really known me,

They'd know that if my life were a car,

Confidence wouldn't be the one driving it.

In fact, confidence wouldn't even be

Sitting in the passenger seat,

For it is fear who sits behind the wheel.

"You've just gotta get over that."

I hear that one a lot,

So I don't talk about my fears anymore.

They're right. I *do* need to get over it,

But could someone at least help me feel understood?

I know that it's normal to be feeling this way,

So why do I feel so alone?

What happened to leaving the light on at night,

And sleeping in their beds when

There were monsters under mine?

Those things were the silly fears,

But now that I'm anxious about

Things even most *adults* are afraid of,

No one's there for me.

I'm trying to confront my fears.

I don't like admitting that I'm afraid to start driving,

But I know that when I finally get it right,

I'll feel like I'm taking a step in the right direction.

My situationship boy repeatedly asks when I'll be getting my license.

"When are you gonna start giving me a ride?" He always asks.

 Beneath the loud environment of our school bus,

I shrug my shoulders.

I don't show it,

But I'm horribly embarrassed.

My dad says that

I'll start driving when he thinks I'm ready.

I know what that means.

That I'm not responsible enough...

I wonder: *How responsible is a sixteen year old girl supposed to be?*

I'm certainly mature *for my age,*

But that doesn't make me any less of a child.

I don't find it insulting,

But rather confusing.

I want to prove myself,

I just don't know how...

I remember what it was like to be little.

As a child,

The aquarium was

Nothing more than a family trip.

I remember pressing my nose up against

The glass of each tank,

Feeling the weight of my own disinterest.

Years slipped by like

Fish darting through water —

Swift and uncatchable.

Now, as a teenager,

Something within me has shifted.

I see beauty in the way fish move —

A harmony that I've never noticed before.

There's a poetry in their movements:

A dance that speaks of

Companionship and simbiosis.

I now realize that the aquarium is not just

A place of observation, but a place of connection.

It's a bridge between my world and theirs.

Within this moment, I find that:

In this world, there's more deeper meanings that

I haven't yet caught onto.

Growing up is nothing but a process.

I can feel the adults in my life resenting me for getting older —

As if they're the only ones grieving who I used to be.

They think I'm in a rush to grow up,

But that couldn't be further from the truth.

They don't seem to understand that:

When I have an attitude,

Or I cry for reasons that may not

Seem important in their world,

I'm really just breaking inside —

Struggling to figure out how

To cope within this new reality of

What it feels like to leave my childhood behind.

My body's changing,

And my mind's still doing it's best to

Swim through thrashing waves of clinical depression.

If I could be a kid for a while longer, I would.

But as I feel the years slipping from my fingertips,

I know it's about time to let go.

It's no one's fault.

It's just the process that's changing me slowly.

Perhaps I'm too naive.

When I'm older,

I'll look back on this and laugh —

Calling my sixteen year old self childish.

I'll sweep the pain of the past beneath the rug,

And forget what it was like to be a moody teen.

The struggle will become a distant memory,

And the adults in my life will accept me as one of them.

When I think of my childhood,

I'll remember the laughs;

Not the times I felt worthless.

Mirrors.

Lately, I don't recognize myself.

Over these past couple of years,

I've seemed to have lost who I am.

I know that it's me who I see in the reflection,

But it almost feels as if I'm looking into the future.

Being sixteen doesn't feel real.

"I don't wanna grow up," I say out loud.

I almost don't realize that I'm crying when I say it.

My mascara runs a little,

And when I go to wipe away the tear,

The blush on my cheek begins to smudge.

I can't remember what age I'd decided that

I needed to wear make-up,

But I know that it's been a routine since then.

I don't look the way I used to,

And I can't quite figure out if

I even remotely like the image of

Whoever it is that I'm looking at now.

Insecurity has a hold on me.

When I'm surrounded by people,

And I look out onto the street,

I never say:

"Oh, she's so fat,"

Or "ew, she's so ugly,"

So why do I find myself

Saying these things when

I look into the mirror?

Why do I hold myself to a different standard —

One that's harsher and less forgiving?

I wonder why I see the flaws that

No one else seems to notice,

And magnify them until

They overshadow the rest of me.

Some of me thinks that:

People would like me more if I was prettier —

That if I were skinnier,

Or had eyes of a different color,

The people who have decided to leave me

Would have chosen to stay instead.

I can't help but to ask those questions.

I always wonder,

If I were more his type,

Would he have hesitated to walk away?

If I were any taller,

And my teeth were more straight,

Would he have decided to stay?

If I didn't have such faded scars,

Or that stupid freckle on my cheek,

Would he have thought twice before leaving me?

If my hair were longer,

And my figure were more petite,

Would he have found me any more complete?

I wonder if I did my make-up like she did,

Or if it weren't for the mole on my leg,

Would he have picked me instead?

These questions haunt my mind,

In search of answers that I'll never find.

I pull myself apart,

Then place the pieces back together like a jigsaw.

I know that I am beautiful.

I deny it when

I'm narrowing myself down to pieces,

But as a whole,

I really am a *stunning* work of art.

Whether or not anyone else notices,

I have the right to feel *gorgeous*.

All the girls he looked at shouldn't matter,

Because they will never be *me*,

And no matter how much of myself

I try to change,

My body and mind are unique.

I shouldn't be worrying about

Whoever might've stayed if I were different,

Because those people are gone for a reason.

The only person I can be is myself,

And I'll never fit into the molds of

Anybody else.

Apologies.

I forgot to block his number.

I didn't *really* forget.

I deleted our texts and pictures,

But I made sure to keep his number in my phone.

You know, just in case he needed anything...

After two years of dating,

It was the least I could do, you know?

Want your stuff back or nah?

I stare at the text in disbelief.

It's been almost a year since we last talked.

Why would I want my stuff back *now*?

I'm certain that he just wants to

Confirm that I miss him,

But I don't... Right?

I stare at the text for a while,

And contemplate how to respond.

> No. Not at all.

I put my phone down.

I take a breath,

But it doesn't help.

Days pass,

And he leaves me on read.

Eventually,

I clear the message,

But something inside of me just

Wants to ask why he *really*

Reached out in the first place.

I sit in my closet and curl into a ball.

I hate having so many things on my mind,

Yet not being able to say a word.

I want to ask how he's doing.

I want to make sure that

He's miserable without me,

And that he's finally gotten

The karma he deserves.

I think of all the times he apologized.

He used to say that I was fragile,

And there's a chance that he was right all along.

I was fragile like paper.

I let his words tear into me,

And his sorrys were like staples.

After being torn,

They'd hold me together for a while,

But with enough rips in my surface,

I began to fall apart.

Staples became useless and outnumbered—

Worsening the damage with the harshest piercings.

Eventually, he ran out of staples,

And had no more left of me to cut.

I may be in pieces,

But I refuse to stay the way he left me.

I use the rest of myself to make tiny origami swans,

And paint the paper a pretty shade of pink.

I will redecorate until he returns,

And when he tries again to staple me,

I will fly far from him.

He no longer has power over me.

Yes, he's permanently changed me,

But I have the power to change myself too —

To grow and become something better,

So in a way,

Thank you.

I tell myself not to cry.

I take another breath,

And block him.

I don't do it because I'm mad,

Or because I'm holding a grudge.

I do it because I know that

Life will only get better when

I stop thinking of him.

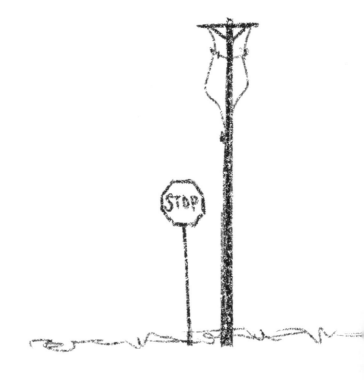

Love.

I like the idea of being loved.

Sometimes, I think of what it'd be like to

Be loved by my situationship boy.

Whenever that thought pops into my head,

I immediately try my best to erase it,

But my mind is like a whiteboard,

And the idea of potential love is

Written in thick, permanent ink.

I don't want to be with anyone, I remind myself.

This morning, I sat down in front of my mirror.

"So what *do* you want?" I asked myself.

To be loved... I thought,

But what confuses me is that:

I *was* loved,

And I threw it away.

I wasn't ready for it.

"So what do you *really* want?" I asked my reflection.

To be loved...

...By you.

"I need to love myself *first*."

I'm learning to *like* myself.

Taking this time to be single is probably

The best thing I've ever done for myself.

Sure, on the outside,

It may have seemed selfish to

Break up with the last boy I dated.

He was nearly perfect —

Nearly everything I could ask for.

But in the long run,

I knew it was better to let him down,

Then to lead him on.

As for my situationship boy,

I think he knows that

We don't really have a chance.

He's already admitted that he likes me,

But says that he'd never date me.

I guess that's fair,

Because I wouldn't have dated him either.

Despite all the things we have in common,

It just doesn't seem like a good idea right now.

I'm not in the position to have a boyfriend,

And he certainly doesn't seem to actually want a girlfriend.

I question myself.

What's keeping me from walking away?

In the very back of my mind,

I think I'm afraid of loneliness.

Even if I don't want to be with anyone,

I'm afraid of a life that lacks

That aspect of romance.

I've always loved the idea of

Getting to know one person,

And taking them on bookstore dates;

Learning all of their favorite things,

And buying them flowers on

Valentine's Day...

Why don't I want to be with anyone? I ask myself.

That's an easy question to answer,

But I don't like admitting it.

I'm afraid of commitment, aren't I?

I wasn't always that way,

I just need to learn how to trust again.

Maybe one day — when I'm healed — I can love someone.

But for now, I'll settle for my situationship boy,

And hope that I don't get too attached.

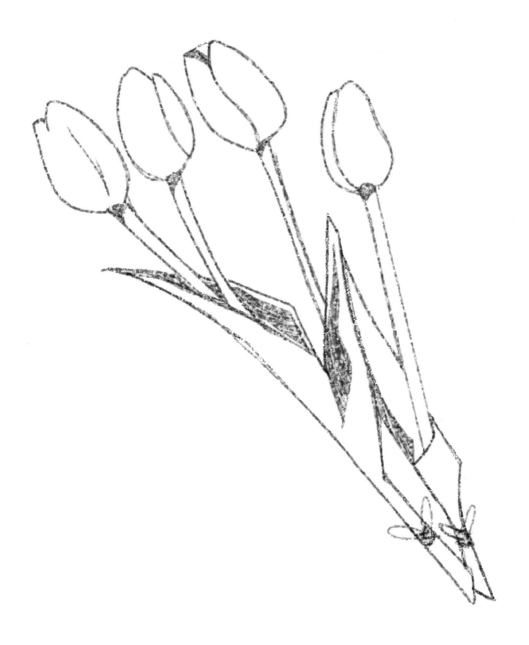

School.

School's out.

My sophomore year felt like a waste.

I feel like I've learned nothing.

These last few months went by in flashes.

I've been living within routine for so long,

That I've forgotten how to actually *live*.

I've just been operating on autopilot;

Spectating my life as it played out before me.

"Today didn't feel like our last day,"

— My situationship boy said to me.

I agree. I feel empty,

As if I've accomplished nothing.

I'm disappointed in myself.

I survived.

That's about all I can say about this school year.

Last year, I nearly ended my life in a bathroom stall.

Undoubtedly, I've grown since then.

Though I may feel empty,

I'm certainly doing better.

I'm okay.

I know that feelings of emptiness often

Accompany transitions,

And that even in moments of uncertainty,

There's always potential for

Growth and new beginnings.

I'm getting stronger, I remind myself.

I'm coping.

I feel dull.

Perhaps it's just loneliness.

I feel as if I've isolated myself from

The rest of the world.

I'm on my own, I think.

I have nobody.

I know it's not true,

But I still can't help but feel it in my bones.

Lately, I spend most of my time outside.

I soak in sun rays,

Wondering why I'm not happy yet.

School's out,

And I'm free,

So why do I feel so trapped?

I'm only a week into the summer.

I've cried so much already.

The stillness of summer gives me more time to think —

To remember everything bad that's ever happened to me.

I'm aware that this is a chance to move forward,

But my mind is at a halt.

I think of my ex, and the girl he left me for.

For only a moment,

I'm mad at the world.

Last summer,

I devoted every second of my time to that boy.

We went on dates,

And when we couldn't see each other,

We texted all day.

I dare to ask myself why this summer feels so different —

So lonely and meaningless,

But I already know the answer.

He's not a part of it anymore.

I try not to think about it.

Besides, I still have my friends.

While they may not provide the

Same comfort that a boyfriend would,

At least I know that they're there for me.

Two weeks of the summer fly by.

I waste my time playing video games.

Really, it's just an excuse to talk to *them*.

I can't call either of them my

"Favorite freshmen" anymore.

They keep reminding me that:

Technically, they're sophomores now.

My situationship boy texts me every morning,

And we converse throughout the day.

When the sun sets,

We pick a random game for all three of us to play.

This process repeats for about a week,

And I begin to think that this summer won't be so bad.

Days pass.

For mornings on end,

I wake up without the usual texts.

The two of them don't ask to talk,

And our usual routine takes a turn.

I find myself wondering what changed —

Why such a familiar silence has settled in.

The laughter and shared moments,

Is now replaced with an empty void.

I hate this feeling.

Last summer,

Everyone blew up my phone —

Asking to hang out,

But this year,

It feels like not even

My only friends want to talk to me anymore.

How do you tell a friend you miss them?

I miss the comfort of knowing they were only a call away.

I realize that it's been a whole month since

Either of them have reached out.

I pick up my phone,

And though there's not a single notification,

It feels too heavy to hold.

How I can I tell them I miss them,

Without sounding needy or desperate?

Honesty is the best approach, isn't it?

I decided to send a simple message to both of them:

"Wanna play something tonight? I miss you guys."

It's a small step, but it's a way to bridge the gap.

I just hope to remind them that

Our friendship is still important to me.

I stare at the screen

I wait for the three dots to signal a reply,

But they never do.

The seconds stretch into minutes,

And I wonder if they even care about me anymore.

Is it possible that I was nothing but a phase within their friendship?

I miss the inside jokes and late night talks.

It's not even the situationship that

I think about anymore —

It's the three of us.

I miss my *friends*.

Sure, I liked the romantic tension,

And the conversations we'd

Have when no one was around,

But when the other told me that

He thought of me as a best friend,

He filled a hole in my heart that

I never even knew existed.

For once in my teenage life,

It felt like there was a boy who

Wanted nothing more than to be my best friend.

I regret becoming so attached.

Now that school's out,

There's no excuse to see each other.

There's no more of that time to kill;

Sitting on our homeroom floor,

Having conversations as we waited for the bell.

I wonder if that's all I was — a way to pass the time.

Maybe it's true:

I was never as important as I thought.

It may sound stupid,

But when I met them at the beginning of the year,

It felt like something within me had shifted —

Become complete.

For whatever reason,

They seemed to look up to me.

When they'd ask me questions,

A sense of pride gathered within me,

And I often began to feel like a mother.

I knew that the feeling was wrong,

But couldn't resist the urge to guide them.

Idiotically, I let that feeling become

A substitute for my sense of purpose.

It just doesn't feel fair.

While I love thinking of the memories we made,

And the times they made me laugh,

I just wish I wasn't here to feel the withdrawal.

The days are long, the nights are cold,

And the echo of their voices still

Lingers throughout my mind.

I want everything back:

The comics I gave away,

And the time I wasted playing random video games.

Perhaps they just realized that I was never really needed —

That I was only good for homework answers,

And to "spice up" life when it got boring.

I'm left with an empty space.

Maybe it's time to accept that things have changed,

And though it may hurt to say goodbye,

Our paths have simply rearranged.

I'll hold onto the experience they provided;

The friendship that at least *felt* true,

And hope that one day,

I'll find a bond that feels *similar* if not

Brand new.

Productivity.

I prioritize my writing.

I pour myself into my work,

But at the back of my mind,

I think of my situationship boy —

How he's seemed to have forgotten me.

It's a constant tug on my thoughts,

Pulling me away from the task at hand.

I try to focus — to lose myself in the details,

But he's always there:

A quiet presence that I can't ignore.

Every now and then,

I catch myself staring blankly at the screen.

I get lost in the memories.

It's both a comfort and a distraction,

This lingering connection...

I wonder if he thinks of me too;

If I cross his mind in the quiet moments of his day.

I shake my head, trying to clear the fog of nostalgia.

There's work to be done, and deadlines to meet.

I try to think of what to write.

I take a deep breath,

Confronting the task at hand.

But no matter how hard I try,

I can't seem to shake the feeling that

A part of me is still with him,

And he'll never take the time to give it back.

I can't stop thinking of him,

And I can't think of what to write,

So I'll compromise with myself.

I'll use this pain to be productive,

And continue to write about him until

The ache in my heart decides to numb.

He lives close to me.

Whenever I pass by his house,

I stick my tongue out and laugh.

I mock him,

Telling myself, *he was never all that.*

But deep down, I know it's all a lie.

It's nothing but a mask to hide the tears I cry.

As I look at that house, I grieve.

I think of the time we had,

And how I wanted him so bad...

It's truly upsetting.

I know he's home,

And always on his phone,

Yet still ignoring the texts I sent so long ago.

I walk by, making childish faces at his window.

Though I know he won't see me,

I hope he feels the negative energy.

I hope he knows just how much I hate him;

That his chances to come back to me are growing slim.

I hope he knows that I won't be

Giving him a ride when I get my license,

And that though I may be grieving his absence,

He will never again feel the warmth of my presence.

Really, I know why he's backing out.

I tend to make him nervous,

And he's said that before.

Perhaps I just make him shy,

So he chooses to ignore.

I know that he's small — smaller than me,

Both physically and mentally.

I'll let him have that for a while longer.

If he's gotten too scared to even talk to me,

It certainly was never meant to be.

I never needed him.

He was never useful,

Or particularly kind,

But for him,

I was both of those things and more.

For him, I offered to do favors,

And would help him with

School work if he asked.

When he was bored,

I was a friend he could call and text.

Now that things have changed,

There's this hole in my heart.

Now, he doesn't even seem to

Want anything to do with me.

At first, I thought I missed him

Because he was so perfect,

But that wasn't the case.

Perhaps I just liked having

Someone to take care of —

To be kind and cater to.

So, no. I didn't need him,

Not at all.

I'm just hurt that

He doesn't need *me* anymore.

Loneliness.

Being alone tears me apart.

It's the first sunny day of July,

And I'm watching the clouds move.

The sky is painted in hues of bright blue —

A stark contrast to the storm brewing inside me.

I close my eyes and take a deep breath,

Hoping to find an ounce of peace within this moment.

I wonder if things will ever change,

Or go back to the way they were.

The silence around me feels heavy;

Almost suffocating.

As mosquitos bite into me,

I become uncomfortable and cold.

I haven't talked much today, I think to myself.

I guess I don't have much to talk about anyway,

Or many people to talk to for that matter...

Suddenly, my jarred up emotions hit me like a bullet train,

And the memories sweep me up like

An uninvited hurricane.

Each memory is vivid.

I close my eyes,

And a single tear escapes.

I wipe it away quickly —

As if denying its existence could

Somehow erase the pain.

"I hate you guys," I say aloud.

No one hears me,

But I wish they could.

"I hate your stupid faces,

And the different smells of your cologne.

I hate the sound of your voices,

And every embarrassing secret ever told."

With tears in both eyes,

I sigh and laugh to myself.

Really, I love *all* those things.

"How stupid that must make me seem, huh?"

The shadows of the trees in my yard seem to stretch,

Creeping closer with every passing second.

I can feel the weight of the silence pressing down on me.

It's a constant reminder that

I'm only good at making friends with loneliness.

Maybe there's something I'm missing...

The more I listen,

The more I realize that it's never been silent out here.

I can hear the buzzing of bees,

The chirping of crickets,

The rustling of leaves,

And the distant hum of cars driving by...

All of these sounds:

A symphony that I've been too distracted to hear.

It's the sound of *life*.

I need to start *living*.

In my lengthy yard,

I listen to music and lay in the grass.

The wind feels like waves on my skin.

I apply my sunscreen and tan,

Absorbing the heat like a sponge.

I sip on ice water, reminding myself to stay healthy.

I cry and wait for the sun to set.

When it does, the streetlights come on,

And the breeze gets colder.

It sends shivers down my spine,

But the goosebumps make me feel alive.

The sky is cloudless,

And the trees become mere silhouettes.

As fireflies drift past me,

I stand from where I'm sitting.

Barefoot and in the dark,

I walk to the middle of my yard.

I freeze there and let the wind nearly knock me over.

"You matter," I say aloud.

"You matter, and someday you'll feel it."

I look at the half moon floating over me,

And only for a second, I feel reborn.

"You matter," I repeat. "You matter."

God.

I believe in God.

My parents were never too passionate about religion,

But I still pray to God every now and then.

I apologize for little things I've done over the years,

And ask God for nothing but forgiveness.

I think I pray to God because of how sorry I am,

Not just to him, but to my parents as well.

Really, I want to apologize for everything,

But I worry that the wrong words will

Leave my mouth — scarring me forever.

I fear that the soil of my sorries won't be

Enough to bury the things I've done,

Or that when I try to apologize,

They won't believe that I truly mean it.

I don't know how to *say* it,

But I *am* sorry,

And no matter what

They may already think of me,

I really *do* care.

I'm sorry.

I'm sorry for my attitude,

And all the times I've slammed a door.

I'm sorry for every argument,

And for the days I was rude to you before.

I'm sorry for going to the counselor's office,

Instead of telling you what was wrong.

Part of me just wanted you to think I was perfect,

And that I've stopped struggling to stay strong.

I'm sorry for never telling you about

The time I went to the nurse's office,

Just to sit behind a curtain and cry.

I'm sorry for my terrible grades,

And every time I've ever lied.

I want you to know that:

Even though I was always relieved to

Get away with certain things,

I was never pleased.

Trust me,

Being this disappointed in myself is

All the discipline I'll ever need.

I feel guilty, even for asking God to forgive me.

I'm crying.

You may not be able to see it,

And you may not believe me either,

But out of every poem in this book,

These ones are the hardest for me to write.

I don't like sleeping.

I'm sorry for sneaking out of the house at night,

Even if I never left the backyard.

When I can't sleep,

I just stand out there and stare at the sky,

Wondering why the hell I'm even alive.

Insomnia roots me to the ground,

And even though I'm tired,

I cannot even think of sleeping.

I'd rather taste the wind,

And wallow in the stings of bug bites.

In the shapes of darkened clouds,

I search for a sign.

Something keeps me awake.

I know it's just my active brain driving me insane,

But as I stand in my backyard's gravel-like pathway,

The thought of throwing myself into the pool settles in.

My father once told me that only cowards commit suicide,

So I have to remind myself that I am no coward.

No matter how scared of myself I may be,

I am not afraid of living.

I lose track of time.

I take a deep breath,

Allowing the cool night air to fill my lungs.

The stars above me are too beautiful to leave behind,

So I convince myself to stay outside a while longer.

The gravel crunches under my feet as I take a step forward,

But I don't violently throw myself into the pool.

Instead, I slip out of my socks,

And take a few steps in.

I stand on the second step,

And let the water engulf my knees.

For no particular reason at all,

I am in pain.

But at the same time,

This is the greatest feeling I've ever felt.

I am alive. I think to myself.

And there's no feeling better than that.

Potential.

I'm somewhat aware of my potential.

It feels like I'm standing at the edge of an ocean.

Waves of different possibilities crash around and into me,

Each one pulling me in a different direction.

I'm uncertain as to when I should *jump,*

And when I should *plant my feet.*

Sometimes I begin to think that

It'd just be easier to let the wave take me.

I know what it's like to count reasons.

I count my reasons to live,

And I have plenty.

I'm happy.

I may not be at complete peace,

But at least I know what it's like to feel joy.

I know the bliss of what it's like to be alive,

So why do I wonder what it'd be like to die?

Why do I invision water in my lungs,

And bullets in my head?

Why do I sometimes wish that when I slept

I'd not wake up because I was dead?

Why do I dream of fire burning into my skin,

Or what it'd feel like if acid seeped in?

Why do I wonder what nothingness feels like when

I have everything around me?

Depression isn't sadness.

Depression doesn't mean I have reasons to die,

I just often crave to know the feeling of it.

Depression is what it feels like to drown despite

Knowing how to swim.

Depression is exhaustion from both good and bad things.

Perhaps I just need to rest, and it will fade.

I was more suicidal than I'd like to admit.

Every now and then,

I'd obsess over the idea of death.

For a long time,

I felt that I truly had no real reason to live.

I looked for it, and it really seemed as if

I wasn't particularly good at anything.

I hated myself;

Not because of any bad aspect in my life,

But because *I* didn't seem to fit in with all the good ones.

I screwed up a lot,

And to be completely honest, I still do.

I was always told that everyone makes mistakes,

But I never really got over the ones I made...

At least I never did drugs, I tell myself.

At least I never snuck out to see a boy,

Or played with matches.

I'm a good kid,

And no one's ever told me otherwise.

Sometimes I just have to remind myself.

I've poured too much of myself into other people.

Listening to their stories,

I've learned something.

In this vast theater of existence,

We all play our parts.

The audience gathers in a dimly lit auditorium.

Some applaud, others hiss, and a few remain indifferent.

I am well aware that I can't make everybody like me,

But I like just about everybody.

Even when their words sting like nettles,

I find solace in their imperfections.

Their rough edges — to me — are only raw materials of humanity.

No one's perfect.

I know that,

So I've never held anyone to that expectation.

People make mistakes — people lie and cheat.

I'd always rather forgive and forget rather than to stop loving.

Somehow, I'm an exception.

Even when I can defend the killer,

And reason with the knives that have stabbed me,

I still find ways to see myself as something worse.

I know that I should learn to love myself before loving anyone else,

But it's hard to love myself when I have no idea who I am.

The water isn't always clear.

The truth is,

We never *find* ourselves,

But rather:

Who we're meant to be finds us.

And when it does,

It's not some magical moment of clarity.

Life is still as unpredictable as it's always been.

It is only when you take the time to

Fulfill your purpose that

Life decides to become easier.

Not because bad things stop happening,

But because you begin to value *yourself* more than

Anything that stands in your way.

I *can* swim.

As I stand at the edge of this vast ocean,

I know that it's okay to feel uncertain.

Each wave is an opportunity;

A chance to learn and grow.

With my priorities in place,

I'm ready to embrace whatever comes my way.

I won't be drowning anytime soon.

Healing.

I am a writer.

I've spent this past year swerving

In and out of relationships,

Trying my best to avoid many,

And working too hard to establish others.

Some were merely pit stops,

While others felt like home,

But one thing I've learned is that:

Almost all people come and go.

I've learned that sometimes,

The heart has a mind of its own,

And no matter how hard I try to protect it,

It will always find a way to feel.

I shouldn't be looking for the perfect people,

Because I know that — right now —

They wouldn't be looking for me.

So before I settle with the perfect person,

I must learn to enjoy my own company.

I've wasted my time chasing closure.

I've finally come to realize that

Closure doesn't reveal itself in

Explanations from the people who've hurt me.

Closure is acceptance within **myself** that those people have changed.

My ex will never be able to undo all the pain he's inflicted on me,

And my situationship boy may never tell me exactly what's on his mind.

My best friends may forget me one day,

And I can't force them to stop drifting away.

I will never be back at my eighth grade desk,

And I can't change anyone else's future.

I can't take back the lies I've told,

Or undo the actions I regret,

But there are a few things I *can* do.

Experience moments as they happen,

Hold onto the memories,

Learn from them,

And move on.

end

ACKNOWLEDGEMENTS:

I may have written and published this book all on my own, but I can certainly say that there have been some extremely important people in my life who have helped make me feel like these big dreams might just be reachable.

Mom & Dad: Thank you so much for supporting me and my wildly ambitious dreams. Your belief in me has been a source of strength and inspiration. I am incredibly grateful for everything you do, and I love you both more than words can express.

My little sister: Thank you for looking up to me even when I didn't have the energy to be kind. I know that you're still small, but I hope that when you're a teen and find yourself struggling to move forward, you'll refer back to my writing and remember that it *does* indeed get better.

My Friends: I don't have many of you, but you guys are all I've ever needed. Thank you all for being my biggest fans, and making me laugh when it felt impossible. Even if we someday part ways, you'll all forever have a special place in my heart. I love you all.

And thank you, **God,** for making this all possible.

Made in United States
Troutdale, OR
08/27/2024

22348177R00058